MAGIC
pen
Emmanuel D.
Nkwenty

AF392187

COPYRIGHT

Published in Nigeria by
Swift Books
an imprint of

Swift Publishers
62, Olawale Street, Ososami,
Oke-Ado, Ibadan, Oyo State.
+2348072970850, +2348157631661
swiftpublishers@gmail.com

ISBN:
978-978-980-729-1

Table of Contents

DEDICATION

To my parents, Chief and Mrs. Okon Jackson Nkanang

ACKNOWLEDGEMENT

Dr. Muneeba Ali Sidique, you have made a bigger impact on me than you realize, and I will tell everyone how amazing you are.

Dr. Enenwan Evanson Aquaowo, you are a very strong woman! God bless you!

Mr. Chandra, when are we having the next cup of tea?

CHAPTER 1

Fabian wasn't a fan of relinquishing his most treasured morning sleep all in the name of going to school. He disliked the idea of waking up early, putting on his green short and white shirt uniform, to face different rules and pressure at school. Between his low grades and everything else, he cringed thinking about leaving the house as he lay carelessly in his bed, enjoying the cool natural air that penetrated his mud fortress through the opened window. He had no idea what time it was, but he was certain his mother would let him know at any moment.

"Fabian!" Mama called softly at first, not showing her true feelings. "Fabian!" She called again; her tone grew a little aggressive, shaking him from his relaxation.

"Yes, Mama!" He answered, as he quickly threw the blanket off his body, wiped the sleep off his eyes, and dashed out of bed with a squeaky sound of relief. He adjusted his hair to make it look like he'd been awake before her arrival. Judging from the sound of her voice, she was very close.

"Fabian!" She called out for the third time, the initial mild knock on the door turned to forceful bangs, as Fabian rushed to the door, held the knob and flung the shaky wooden door open to greet her.

Scared, he fumbled with his clothes and tried to look her in the eyes. "Mama! G...oo...dmor...ning. I woke up a long time ago!" He stammered helplessly through his lie.

"Fabian! It is 7:15 on a Monday morning and you are still sleeping! Are you not going to school?" She demanded.

"I will, Mama." He wanted to feel bad for disappointing her, but he really didn't want to go.

"Then why didn't you wake up before now? Didn't you hear when the cock crow?"

In this part of Africa, cock crow was a wake-up alarm, and for someone like Mama. Whenever the first cock crowed, that's when her morning starts.

"Mama, no cock has crowed today. I'm suspecting they were overfed yesterday, so they are too lazy to crow today." Just then, a cock ran out of the bush and crowed, not just once, but thrice, and

Fabian lowered his eyes in shame as he walked past Mama to start his only morning chores – sweeping.

"Drop that broom and go have your bath before I lose my temper this morning!" She fussed.

He obediently went straight to the bathroom to get started. Apart from moments like this, Mama was the most caring, loving, and hardworking being Fabian knew. She had a housekeeping job with the local government miles and miles away which was on a part-time basis, and every day when she came home from that job, she engaged in subsistent farming. The proceeds of all of her jobs were used in running the home.

Mama was the only parent he knew, his Father had left the village in search of greener pastures in the city when Fabian was just one year old and since then he never returned and no one heard anything from him. Being a fairly educated man, he rooted for a foreign name for his first child and listened with amusement as Mama and the locals had difficulties in pronouncing it; but over the years, only Mama seemed to have mastered its pronunciation, while the locals still struggle; calling him *"Abian"* as against *Fabian*. Fabian had not felt the absence of a father figure in his life and he had never given such thing a thought because Mama was always there to take care of his every need. For the 14 years of Fabian's short life, he couldn't remember a single time he felt hungry or disgraced at school for lack of payment of any fee. She'd also promised to sponsor his education to any level, but Fabian didn't see that possibility because he had no aspiration of going further, academically.

———

After Fabian finished bathing, he did not come out of the bathroom, but when it dawned on him that Mama will come calling any moment, he sluggishly came out. His breakfast was waiting for him, as well as his school uniform.

That Monday morning, just like every other school day, was not going well for Fabian, his desire to shun school has always met Mama's wrath.

"Eat very fast, so you can catch up with your colleagues!" Mama ordered. "You are in SS1, and yet, you don't know the value of education, not to talk of having a dream." She added.

"Mama, I have a dream. I even had one this morning before you came to wake me." He said as he bit into his food.

She shook her head at his ignorance. "I pray one day you will see things my way."

"Mama, can I ask you a question?"

"Go ahead."

"What do I need school for?"

"Fabian!" She sighed. The question was his most frequently asked question, and she was clearly tired of it. "As I always say, this is your formative years. I can't teach you all that you need to know, that's why I send you to school so you can learn other things to compliment my effort."

"Just that?"

"And besides, I send you to school to get education, and do you know what education is?" She didn't take a pause before answering her own questions. "Education is the passport to the future, for tomorrow belongs to those who prepare for it today."

"Ok! Did you go to school?"

"I didn't have such opportunity."

"Now I offer you an opportunity. Take my uniform, go and replace me in school please."

"I don't want to continue this discussion with you."

"You wear my uniform and go, while I stay at home." He pushed his luck.

"Shut up!"

"You see? Even you don't like school!"

Her look became fierce and Fabian got the message immediately. It was time to keep quiet, finish the food, jump into his school uniform and leave for school as soon as possible.

~

IkotObong Akan Community High School sat on a forty acre of land, just a stone throw away from Fabian's house. All the on-going activities in the school could always be heard from his house. Several times, Mama had told Fabian the story of how his grandfather donated much of his farmland so the state government could create the school in their community. His gesture received a lot of commendations locally and outside the community, but it always puzzled Fabian. He always wondered how a nobleman like his grandfather could do such a thing to his grandson. How could he have conspired with the government to build a prison for him, where he was stripped of his rights and freedom, where he had to be taught how to walk, talk, dress, and behave?

When he finally got to school, his mind drifted off immediately; Biology class dragged on until his prayers were answered. The teacher, Mrs. Udofia, wrapped up the topic, packed her things, and left the class early. Immediately, the rowdiness of conversations and laughter got louder with each passing second. The boys, who had paused their police and thief game when Mrs. Udofia came in, continued from where they stopped, while the girls picked up their gossip again.

Musa and Stanley, Fabian's two close buddies went to the front of the class to continue their paper soccer game, raising dust from the damaged cemented floor to the atmosphere. Fabian stayed in his seat and watched as they displayed their skills. They signaled him to join them, but he waved them off. Moments later, Musa scored an obvious goal, but Stanley denied the ball ever made it through the caricature goalpost, they argued for a while before going to Fabian to decide their fates.

"Fabian, was that not a goal?" Musa asked while Stanley smilingly winked at Fabian from Musa's back to favour him in his decision.

"I don't know." Fabian replied, not wanting to take sides. His mood hadn't started off great in the morning and had only dampened by the punishment he received at the school gate for coming late. The school principal gave him six strokes of his cane, which had left his palm bruised.

Stanley and Musa usually made school fun for Fabian, the three of them were a perfect gang. Stanley was the physical and aggressive one that always got his matching orders from Fabian who was deemed to be the master mischief plotter. Though, of the same age, Fabian had proven himself worthy to be obeyed. Musa was the passive guy who was neither here nor there, without them attending school with Fabian each day; truancy would have been a good idea to him. They even called themselves the three musketeers or the big boys; they claimed to control every student in the school and any student that didn't want to be under their control met Stanley's wrath.

Their seats were at the back and it was a no-go area for the frail. Nearly all troubles in the class were attributed to them; both students and teachers alike knew the group as the most unserious.

"Fabian, we all know you're not happy about something, and since you have refused to tell us about it, let us add to the list of your unhappiness. The examination timetable is out." Musa said, when he noticed his dampened spirit. "And Ifiok has threatened to boycott our agreement if we don't increase his daily pay." He added.

The examination timetable being released was not a big issue to Fabian, he knew how every examination ended, he knew his position in class, and Mama seemed to have gotten used to his academic failure. So, he clearly ignored the threat and focused on the problem that actually meant something to him.

"He raised the price again? What does he take us for? A bank?" Fabian spewed his displeasure.

"Not just an ordinary bank, bro. He thinks we are Central Bank." Musa answered while taking the seat opposite Fabian.

"That is why we have to act tough. We should just handle this boy, beat him up after class today and then, we won't need to pay anymore and he'll never have the guts to answer any question in this class."Stanley contributed as he abandoned the paper ball on the floor and took a seat beside Musa.

"Shhhhh! Bring down your voice. Have you forgotten what the school authority did to us when they learned that we used to bully him?" Fabian cautioned.

"That is why we have to lure him outside the school. If you guys don't want to get involved, I can beat him all by myself. I will wait for him after school hours and decimate him." Stanley whispered as he put his fist into his hand in a fierce way. As the strongest amongst them, whenever there was a need for physical attack on students, Stanley always took the front seat. Coincidentally, Ifiok was always at the receiving end until it backfired and led them into trouble with the school management.

"Stanley's right. Let's teach this bookworm a lesson he won't forget in a long while." Musa concurred.

"Guys! Let's take some time and mull over our options." Fabian suggested, not wanting them to get in more trouble than normal.

"Oh, that's one thing I don't like about you Fabian! What are we even thinking about right now? It's obviously time to beat up this guy. He's just bad to us always." Stanley voiced out in frustration.

"Stanley, I will ignore that, but whatever we have to do, let's do it before the commencement of the exams."

Ifiok was the most brilliant student in their class. Term after term, he topped the class in all examinations and class works. He was simply every teacher's favourite and usually answered their questions correctly because he studied and paid attention, while everyone else messed around. Due to his hard work, he seemed to know everything which created problems for Fabian and his gang.

Since Ifiok's success in class, most teachers adopted the belief that Fabian and his gang were not taking their studies seriously and deserved to be punished. In an effort to stop the punishments, they decided to bully Ifiok to silence his brilliance. The school authority learned of their bullying and dealt with them, so they stopped for a while. After some time, they tried to play it safe and came up with the idea of paying Ifiok a daily stipend to keep his mouth shut whenever any teacher asked questions in class. Ifiok's participation fell off in school and their punishments decreased. It was time to handle Ifiok squarely, since he had become an Oliver Twist - always asking for more.

When Stanley and Musa walked away from Fabian's seat to start another game, Fabian knew the burden of handling Ifiok's excesses rested on him solely. He allowed Ifiok's puzzle to dominate his mind and his decision not to join his friends in the game aided his thoughts, Offering him an increment was completely out of his options.

When he finally got it figured out, it was like a veil removed from his eyes, his eyes brighten and his spirit elevated, he clenched his teeth and punched the air in excitement; *"keep your friends close and your enemies closer."* His inner voice whispered to him. *"Yes!*

That's it! That's the mistake I have made all along and I will correct it." He assured himself.

His plan was still skeletal though, he needed more time to add flesh to it, until then, he had to maintain the status quo. He reached out to Stanley and Musa for their own daily stipend and he sent it to Ifiok as part of their agreement.

Their agreement was put to test once again; when Mr. Okafor, the English teacher came into the class. After some minutes of teaching, he threw several questions at the class, the whole class kept mute; no student made any attempt, not even the all-knowing Ifiok.

"Have I not taught stress pattern in this class?" Mr. Okafor shouted out of frustration.

"Nooooo!" The students chorused, Fabian and his boys at the back screamed the loudest and even waved their hands to show total disapproval.

"I am very sure I did." Mr. Okafor said. Out of the blues, Stanley raised his hand calling Mr. Okafor's attention.

"Yes, Stanley! You have something to say?" "Yes! I remember you taught us Stress Pattern sir." His statement startled the whole class as they all turned and looked at him where he stood; they never expected it from him.

"Good boy! Now remind your colleagues what we said on that day."

"Sir, Stress Pattern is defined as pathways through which stress moves into our body."

"Come again!" Mr. Okafor said in total disbelief and awe, as Stanley repeated himself.

"Oh my God! This is unbelievable... Ok, can you give an example?"

"Yes, I can. Sir, from what I have personally noticed and what my friends have told me, the stress pattern amongst students is by waking up early and coming to school. Musa, Fabian am I right?" Though Musa and Fabian were not sure, but they managed to nod their heads in agreement.

"Please, class clap for him." Mr. Okafor urged the class, and with excitement, the class gave a thunderous applause.

"You are all zombies! Zombies of the highest caliber." There was a thick quietness in the class as Mr. Okafor paced in his confusion.

"I have being a teacher for twenty years of my life, what does that tell you? Teaching is more than a profession to me. It is my destiny! During these twenty years, I have seen kids that started on the wrong footing, messed up their lives and still make something good with their lives at the end. So, no matter how much you frustrate me, I will not give up on any of you. There is still hope! I am very sure there is hope for all of you... I have taught Stress Pattern over and over in this class? Stanley, how can you say you get stressed when you come to school? Are you coming to school for me? Definitely no, not even for your parents. You are coming here to get educated so your chances of succeeding in life would be increased. Well, since you all said I haven't taught Stress Pattern in this class, no problem. But don't be surprised to see it in your examination. Goodbye!" He left the class.

As expected, the class became rowdy again; Fabian and Musa stood up and hailed Stanley for his courage in frustrating Mr. Okafor.

"If you cannot hail me again, 'don't be surprised to see it in the exams'." Stanley made jest of Mr. Okafor and his friends laughed heavily.

"Talking about exams, we need to do something fast." Fabian said when the laughter subsided.

"We have to secure the Magic Pen." Musa followed up.

"How can we, when everyone is pretending not to know anything about the existence of such a pen?" Stanley asked.

"You can't blame them; the pen is such a secret."

"Once we lay our hands on the pen, this exam would be over before it begins."

"It will save us from reading." Musa said.

"Exactly!" Fabian concluded.

It was 12noon when the school bell rang out, dismissing everyone for lunch. Fabian and his gang were the first to leave the class.

At the cafeteria, the only thing that mattered to Fabian was Ifiok, he kept his eyes on him while he also hurried Stanley and Musa to finish their snacks and follow him back to the class. He was eager to kick-start the implementation of his new plan, he became restless when he got to the class, pacing from one end of the class to another, putting his words together. When Ifiok returned from the cafeteria,

Fabian quickly led him to a corner of the class then signaled Musa and Stanley to join him and they did, unaware of his intentions.

"But I haven't answered any questions."Ifiok trembled as he was being taken away.

"Keep quiet! You this good-for-nothing piece of shit." Stanley ordered.

"You want an increment huh? You will get an increment." Musa said.

"By the time we are done with you, you will regret every dime you took from us." Stanley continued.

From their body language, Stanley and Musa clearly misunderstood Fabian's game plan and were ready for a physical assault on him. Fabian kept quiet and listened to them rant, he knew none of them will hit him without his consent.

"This time around, we are going to beat you to a pulp and no teacher will come to your rescue." Stanley maintained.

"Exactly!" Musa concurred.

When Fabian noticed Ifiok's eyes were shimmering with tears, he broke his silence.

"Hey guys chill! We are not here to beat anyone. Do you believe me Ifiok? I brought you here to give you an offer that will change your life completely." Fabian finally opened up.

"If this is about the increment I asked, please I don't want it anymore."Ifiok Stammered.

"No! It's not, Ifiok. I want you to be our friend." Fabian said.

Fabian's declaration startled Stanley and Musa; their eyes probed Fabian's face like a mind-reader machine.

"Wait, let us understand one thing. Fabian you want Ifiok to be our friend?" Musa demanded, as Fabian nodded in affirmation.

"Be whose friend?" Stanley demanded with anger.

"Fabian, I didn't expect this from you. You are joking, right?" Musa asked.

"That will never happen." Stanley continued to rage.

"How do you expect this low life dude with no class to be rolling with us?" Musa queried.

"You guys should chill. I got this." Fabian said, as he turned to them and noticed the disappointment on their faces.

"See what I said? Fabian is too weak, especially when it comes to dealing with Ifiok." Stanley said to Musa.

"Fabian! What are you doing? He will ruin our reputation." Musa said.

"Do you want to beg this book rat? Go ahead, but just count me out..." Stanley delivered his last words and left.

"Fabian, are you sure of this?" Musa asked.

"Trust me! I got this Musa." Fabian replied.

"Ok! If you say so." Musa left as well. Then, Fabian turned to a feeble-looking Ifiok who could not even maintain eye contact.

"I want you to be close to us. I want you to roll with us and do the things we do. It will be an added advantage to you." He continued. "Look at yourself, you are brilliant and intelligent, but you don't enjoy yourself; no social life, as all you do is to study, move around with big textbooks, from school to your house, and then back to school again. You are pathetic, and you are completely unfair to yourself."

He kept mute for the message to sink. "I bet, you have one or two things to learn from us, and in case you don't know, all the girls in this school are in love with you and we are your only chance of getting them."

Immediately he mentioned the girls part, Ifiok raised his head up, his eyes brightened, becoming very attentive and interested.

"Really?" He asked and Fabian knew he has struck a chord, so he pushed further.

"Yes! I can woo any girl in this school for you; just the other day, Yemi asked us to invite you to her village yam festival, but we didn't know if you were going to be interested, so we decided not to take you along, and you missed a great deal of fun. Just yesterday, Chidinma told me how much she likes you. So you see? The girls them want you."

"So you mean, if I join you guys, I will get any girl I want?" Ifiok finally found his voice.

"Yes! Just come out of your shell." Fabian answered immediately.

"Stanley and Musa seem not to be in consonant with you on this." Ifiok said.

"Don't worry your head about that, I will handle them."

Before Fabian could bring him to either accept or decline his offer, he noticed other students scrambling to their seat at the sight of Mr. Williams, the Mathematics teacher, walking down like an enraged bull. They also scrambled as fast as they could to their seats.

Mr. Williams walked into a calmed and organized class as the students stood to greet him; he gestured them not to bother. He knew he was twenty minutes late and needed to make the best use of the remaining minutes, according to him; he had so much to cover. Mr. Williams was also a no-nonsense teacher, a disciplinarian that brought out the best behaviour in the students. Without wasting time, he picked up the chalk the class captain had placed for him and wrote *"Simultaneous Equation"* on the black board.

After some examples and explanation, he gave a class work and asked if there was any student amongst them that could solve it, and everyone pointed at Ifiok. "Of course, it has to be Ifiok." Mr. Williams said as he gestured Ifiok to come forward.

Ifiok turned and looked at Fabian, seeking approval from him; Fabian gave him a thumps up before Ifiok proceeded to solve the equation.

Meanwhile, Mathematics had being Ifiok's problem, as his performance in most of his examinations had been foiled by his Mathematics result. He knew he wasn't good at Mathematics and he was quietly working to upturn the tide. As Ifiok got to the board, collected the chalk and started solving the equation with a trembling hand, Fabian sat quietly to observe if his hard work has started yielding positive results, but all he could noticed was his heart beating very fast and his sweat gland secreting at a faster pace too. Whatever he was writing seem like gibberish to Fabian, but Mr. Williams kept approving him with nods, after some erasing here and there. He arrived at the answer and Mr. Williams turned to ask the whole class;

"Is he correct?"

"Yesss!" The whole class echoed confidently, falling for the same trap again. Why won't they since it was the all-knowing Ifiok that solved it and they also caught Mr. Williams nodding his head in agreement from time to time.

"You are all morons!" A frustrated Mr. Williams resorted.

"So you people just sat there, acting like you understand all along, but in reality, none of you understands this simple thing. Shame on you all!"

A cold chill gripped the whole class as the students quietly prayed the situation doesn't escalate into a punishment.

"Even you Ifiok, you have being rumoured to be one of the best students in this school... well (he shrugged) I am not surprised; most rumors have always being wrong when put to the test."

He snatched the chalk from Ifiok, solved the equation and explained it all over again, as Ifiok quietly walked back to his seat with a deflated ego.

"Is this equation too hard?" Mr. Williams asked when he arrived at the answer and nobody dared to answer him.

"The problem with you all is that, you don't go back home to study, once you're done in school, it's always a festival back home. See, every time you refuse to learn, you surrender your critical weapon to lead in your generation to the few group of people who always learn, then in the nearest future, you'll summit your CV to them for employment."

He dropped the chalk on the floor and walked out of the class; surprisingly, the class didn't go into frenzy as usual.

It was obvious how defeated Ifiok felt as he buried his head on his desk, so Fabian thought it would be unwise to summon him again and conclude their earlier discussion. He gave up hope of striking the deal with him that day, but to his surprise, Ifiok walked up to him with clenched teeth, indicating his determination.

"Will you woo any girl I point at for me?"

"Yes!" Without a second thought, Fabian answered.

"Then I will be your friend." He stretched his hand for a handshake.

"Deal?"

"Deal."

Without hesitation, Fabian created a space for Ifiok at the back of the class and convinced him to move his seat to the back of the class; he even helped him move his belongings. He went further to offer him a bean cake, the extra one he bought during lunch time. Ifiok was stunned at the turn of events; *why has Fabian become so nice to me? A piece of the puzzle is missing.* He thought as he sat in his new seat and munched his bean cake.

Even though Stanley and Musa still did not understand why Fabian required Ifiok to join their group, since they trusted Fabian's sense of judgment, they accepted Ifiok into their fold whole-heartedly and they became a perfect gang of four. They spent most of their time that day talking about games, village festivals, girls, fashion, entertainment icons, music, etc. To their amazement, Ifiok knew quite a few, and his social skills were not as bad as they had thought. His friendship with Ifiok got deep with each passing minute, and the earlier apprehension Ifiok had faded away, but he needed to be sure.

"Why are you guys so nice to me all of a sudden?"Ifiok was forced to ask.

"Ask Fabian." Musa answered pointing at Fabian.

"What? Don't you like it this way?" Fabian countered.

"I do. It's just strange to me. Some moments ago, none of you would have had anything to do with me, but all of a sudden, here we are discussing as if we have been friends for years."

"Well, I just felt we should not be hostile to you anymore." Fabian answered.

With such an answer, Ifiok knew there was more to it and he had to thread with caution, even if his earlier apprehension has faded.

In preparation for the fourth coming examinations, all the teachers needed to complete their syllabus and assessment. So, series of tests were announced in the class; the class captain came into the class carrying a bunch of Mathematics test scripts they had taken the previous day and started calling out names, but his voice was overwhelmed by the noise and disturbance till Fabian came to his rescue, he hit the table three times and called for calmness and attention. The class settled before the class captain continued calling the names all over again.

"Once you hear your name, come out to get your script." He announced.

The failure was en-masse, as no student was spared. When Fabian got his script, he was not moved because he was used to failing after all. He only waited for Ifiok to get his script so he can see his score. To his surprise, when Ifiok got it, he also failed, but he wasn't moved as well; he only glanced at the score, squeezed the script, threw it out of the window and continued his rubber band war with Musa and Stanley.

"So, now that we are friends, will you still collect the daily stipend from us?" Fabian asked as he joined the rubber band war.

"I knew all along that's what this is all about."Ifiok said, and they both laughed.

"Oh Ok! You caught me there."

"Fabian, I can read your mind and I know you so well."Ifiok said.

"Fabian, is it true?" Musa enquired.

"Yes."

"Ifiok, if you knew all along, why did you still accept his friendship offer?" Stanley asked.

"Well, I was not comfortable getting money from you guys anymore."

"But you asked for increment."

"I knew you guys can't afford raising the stakes, so it was my way of saying I'm not for sale anymore."

"Wow, you two are playing mind games, huh?"

"In fact, hence forth, you guys don't need to give me money anymore, all I just need from you guys is to help me woo a girl; I need a girl as soon as possible."

"You must really be serious about having a girlfriend; do you have any girl in mind?" Fabian asked.

"Yes!"

"...And who is that unfortunate girl?" Musa asked.

"Unfortunate?" Ifiok smilingly asked, and they all laughed again.

"When you guys are done laughing, write down this name; Ima Benson!"

"Which Ima Benson?" Stanley queried.

"The same one you guys know in SS2." He responded casually and everyone got serious.

"Dude, are you out of your mind?" Musa asked.

"Ima Benson is a class higher than you; she is not in your level, and definitely not your kind of girl. Common bro, look for some other girl." Stanley corrected.

"See, I know we have said you are now a big boy, but you are taking this too far." Musa said.

"You said you were going to woo any girl for me once I join you; so, it's either Ima Benson or I call off this deal."

"Ok! Ok! Ok! Chill bro! I will work out something for you." Fabian rushed to salvage the deal.

Ima Benson was a class higher than them, and she was the most brilliant girl in the entire school. She had represented the school in all inter-school competitions and had won laurels after laurels for the school. For that, every teacher, including the principal, adored and respected her. From what Fabian knew of her, she was a snob and does not interact with people beneath her level. Fabian was convinced she was going to turn Ifiok down, but to keep his side of the deal, he had to try.

"Ok! Is that settled?" Ifiok asked Fabian.

"Yes! I will get you Ima Benson." Fabian said.

"Then, let's go play game in school two." Ifiok said and they were surprised to hear that from him but they tried not to show it.

"Yes! Let's go there." Musa concurred.

"We will also watch some movies." Stanley said.

"I go with Stanley." Fabian said.

"Whatever you intend to do, let's just leave this boring class." Ifiok said.

"Ifiok, the school gate would be locked; how do you suggest we leave the school premises?" Fabian asked with a little smile.

"You really must think I'm a novice." Ifiok answered smilingly.

"How do you mean?"

"You think I don't know you guys jump the perimeter fence when going to school 2?" Ifiok exposed.

They busted into laughter as they walked to their seat to get their bags and went out of the class to a deserted school field. Other students were in their respective rowdy classes while others were occupied by teachers. Bending their heads, they sneaked through those classes occupied by teachers; tried so hard not to make a sound or attract any attention as they head toward the soccer field. Fabian peeked at the school gate; it was locked as expected, and at that point, there was no excuse whatsoever that would make the security man open it. They carefully avoided the gate and headed straight to the corner of the fence that was close to school 2. They observed the environment to be sure no one was looking in their direction. Then, they walked erect; before Fabian could give them signal to jump, Ifiok stylishly somersaulted to the other side of the fence and landed with a loud crashed sound. Musa and Stanley turned to look at Fabian in fear;

"Ifiok are you okay?" Fabian whispered.

"Can't you girls jump?" Came his reply.

"Oh, he's still alive." Stanley said.

Since becoming Fabian's friend, Ifiok became daring, sophisticated and even threatening Fabian's leadership role of the group. The message was clear; things have changed and they have changed so fast, not the same cool-headed bookworm anymore. Fabian was the last to jump and he did so to the observing eyes of the other three guys. His landing made it obvious who the real boss was as he couldn't maintain balance. He got ashamed and couldn't utter a word, neither could Stanley and Musa. Like a sheep following his shepherd, they quietly followed Ifiok's leadership. For them not to be caught, Ifiok avoided the major road leading to School 2 and took them through a bush path, one that is not known to his new friends.

"Ifiok, how come you know this route to school two?" Musa queried.

"Because I don't come to school 2 does not mean I don't know different routes."

School 2 was a name given to a mini shopping mall with 12 outlets that housed games like snooker, betting shop, candy shop, toy shop, restaurant, bookshop, etc., and was located close to *IkotObong Akan community High school.* The mini mall was a tourist site for the recalcitrant students, as they visit there during or after school hours for all sorts of games.

When Ifiok led them to school 2, Itoro, the game centre attendant was just coming out of his shop as if to receive them; Fabian exchanged pleasantries with him, and then introduced him to their new recruit Ifiok. Itoro took them into his store, and immediately set up the video game and handed over the game pads to Fabian. Gradually, Fabian's confidence returned and he was determined to regain his lost pride, the one he lost some minutes ago to Ifiok. He was very good at video games; he chose Ifiok as his first opponent and pleaded with Stanley and Musa to stay and watch. He was very sure of his skills and needed to show Ifiok who the real boss was. After He defeated Ifiok 4 consecutive times, his bragging right returned. Before he moved on to defeat Stanley and Musa.

While Fabian was busy defeating others, Ifiok excused himself out of the game centre for a long time, only to return looking completely different. His bogus uniform was slim fit to meet modern day fashion; his usual low cut hair style was changed to something like a rock and roll star. He sagged his school pants to fit his bouncy walking steps, and also popped his collar. Fabian, Musa and Stanley were stunned to see him that way; they paused the game and carefully observed him from head to toe with their mouth ajar.

"What? Haven't you guys seen a pop star before? Or you need an autograph?"Ifiok questioned.

"Yes! This is how you should be looking." Fabian said, as they stood and took turns to shake hands with him.

"You look great man." Musa complimented.

"The only thing missing right now is a girlfriend." Ifiok said.

"Yes! You're damn right." Fabian concurred.

With the whole transformation in a day, Fabian knew he had gotten Ifiok where he wanted. He knew his popularity amongst students and teachers will soar, and everyone will want to mingle with him and the distraction from his studies would be unprecedented.

They continued their games and kept losing to Fabian while he fed on their frustration, but one thing was certain, Ifiok was becoming a potent threat to his dominance each time they played.

CHAPTER 2

It was 6pm when Fabian and his friends came out of School 2, set to go home; without saying much, they shook hands, greeted and headed in different directions. The roads were deserted and school had closed long ago. It was an eventful day as everything had worked perfectly well for Fabian, and his excitement knew no bounds and couldn't make him behave like a senior student that he was, as he kicked pebbles, creating a huge ball of dust behind him. A fifteen-minute walking distance from the game centre to his house was reduced to ten minutes, but not without sweating and panting. He only realized the extent of his actions when he got to the bamboo gate of his house; he stopped and looked behind to see if anyone, especially any junior student, had seen him misbehave. He was lucky none saw him; otherwise, he would have been ridiculed the next day at school. As he pushed open the bamboo gate, it dawned on him that he had missed his daily ritual; he didn't take some time to observe the bamboo perimeter fence if it has been breached by any roaming goat or ram.

Just like other houses in the village, Fabian's house was made of mud, but new. After years of living in a wretched one, Mama made a commitment to build a new one before the next rainy season and Fabian personally did the finishing and designs; adorned it with beautiful flowers to the admiration of the villagers. There was no passer-by who never gave the house a second look.

After he realized the fence was intact, he walked into the compound and felt Mama's presence as her room was opened. He ignored his own quarters and went straight to Mama's deserted room, quietly kept his bag, then tiptoed to where he expected to see her; as expected, she was in the kitchen. He made a funny sound to startle her, but she wasn't in any way alarmed, she only managed a soft smile.

"I heard your footsteps." She said while still washing the plates.

"Oh my shoes gave me off, I guess."

She observed him. "You are panting and sweating, you must have been running."

"Yes! Good afternoon Mama. Let me help you with those plates."

"That's my good son. Come and sit."

"Common Mama, you know I was joking." They both laughed.

"Lazy boy, go to your room and change your clothes because of this smoke."

"Mama I heard people in the city don't use fire wood to cook."

"I don't know son, since I haven't gone to the city before."

Cooking with firewood is as ancient as *IkotObong Akan* village itself, to reduce the harmful effect of the smoke; Mama told the builders to separate the kitchen from the main building and mandated them to make it as simple as possible. It wasn't anything close to fancy, it was a 4 strong wood rooted firmly in the ground with thatched roof; no wall, no design, just a rope tied from one wood to the other so she could hang her corn to dry for the next planting season. With this kind of structure, the breeze determined the direction of the smoke and Fabian seemed to be attractive to it.

"Fabian, go inside! This smoke is too much." Mama insisted and Fabian finally obeyed.

As he walked through her room again, heading to his quarters, he noticed his past examination result displayed on her bed, then, it dawned on him that Mama had gone through them again. This got him jittery and a deep sadness laced with guilt gripped him. He knew what was coming next, so he immediately went straight to his door, unlocked it, went inside, and deliberately spent more time than expected in his room.

After sometime, Mama didn't see him come out; she called out as loud as she could;

"Fabian! Come out and get your food."

"I'm not hungry Mama." He replied, trying to avoid the tongue lash that will exude in the process of eating, but this did not go down well with Mama as she came to his room and picked a seat beside his bed.

"Why are you not hungry? Are you sick?"

"No Mama. I am not sick."

"Then why are you not hungry?"

"Mama, I'm fine."

"Come out and eat; I made your favourite." She stood and gently pulled him out of the bed. He reluctantly followed her and was unnerved when he noticed Mama had removed his results.

She had prepared *Afang* Soup, with *Fufu* to go with it; carefully placed on the small table with the steam helping to spread the aroma of the stockfish, all over the room. It was the type of meal that never escaped Fabian's compliment, but that day, he quietly devoured it. After some minutes, more than half of it was gone. He was filled, but *Fufu* was still in the plate, so he summoned the courage to finish it. After he was done, he sat there, picking his teeth and thinking how lucky he was to have a mother as his. He had heard people used fancy words to describe their mother, but for him, he always resisted such temptation, no amount of fancy words was ever good enough to describe Mama. Her love for him was something that he could not explain; it was made of deep devotion and sacrifice. Despite all the heart breaks and disappointments he caused her, she was always patient when he was foolish and source of his strength when he was weak; because of her unquenchable believe in him, she never stopped being his greatest fan. If he had his choice of mothers, she was the one he would choose over and over again.

As he sat completely relaxed and oblivious of his surroundings, Mama walked in unnoticed and slammed the bunch of his past results on the floor, he was startled and she took the seat close to him.

"This is it, the very tongue lash I have been avoiding". He tried to dodge.

"Oh! Thank you Mama. It was delicious as always." He complimented the meal he just finished.

"Thank you my son. Are you sure you are satisfied?"

"Yes Mama!" He immediately carried the tray of plates and stood up to leave, trying to avoid the discussion.

"Let me wash these plates outside."

"No. Not yet." She replied.

"I also want to wash my school uniform, socks, sweep the floor and the whole compound. What else will you want me to do?"

"Take a seat." Mama calmly said.

"Oh! I should take the seat alone? That's no problem, I will also wash it." He carried the seat.

"Fabian, I know you saw this discussion coming, so sit down."

"Ok! Can I at least pee outside?"

"No."

He completely ran out of tricks; he just had to face it once and for all, as he dropped his overfed self into the seat, and Mama started.

"It is every parent's duty to make sure that his or her family is happy. You are my son and my family; everything I have done and will do is for your happiness or are you not happy?"

"Mama, I am happy."

"Good. Am I happy with you?"

"I don't know Mama." He replied casually, but deep down in his heart, he knew Mama wasn't happy with his academic performance.

"You were just one year old when your Father left for the city, since then I have not seen him or heard from him. no message from him or any contact with him. I don't know if He is alive or not, I don't know if he will ever come back... I am trying my best to give u a life I never had...You must have noticed; I went through your past results and it worries me. I am not happy with your academic performance, despite the sacrifices I put up. Look at this (she picked one out of the bunch and showed him) 9 subjects and you failed all; same here, same here, here (she kept smashing the result sheet one after the other on the floor as if she was playing cards) and here. The only thing written with blue ink is just your name." She got tired and discontinued. Fabian felt her frustration, but as usual, he had to say something in his defense.

"Mama, teachers these days don't use blue pen to record scores anymore, they prefer red pen, especially when recording examination scores." She shook her head in pity and quietly picked one of the results.

"And I guess the teachers also prefer recording 0/10 in continuous assessment and 5/60 in examination?" Her rhetorical question sealed his lips and Mama continued. "Just as I keep telling you, I never had the opportunity of going to school or learn new skills, but you do; utilize it, build yourself and it would improve your chances of being successful in life. I know you don't like school, but you just need to because school is a place that offers education to people and education is the passport to the future; tomorrow belongs to those who prepare for it today. Just pick Ifiok as a case study; have you not seen his academic performance? He keeps getting better every term."

"Talking about Ifiok, Mama you know his parents really contributed to his success academically."

"How do you mean?"

"His parents named him Ifiok, which means wisdom in our dialect, and wisdom is a higher form of knowledge, so you see? If you had named me Ifiok or something related, I would have being knowledgeable as well."

"Ok."

"And again, Ifiok has a big head that enables him store as many information as possible, if you had made my head big when I was a little, it would have helped me also because the size of the head is directly proportional to the amount of the information a student can store."

At this juncture, Mama didn't know when her jaw dropped

"Fabian are you serious?"

"Mama I'm serious." She was short of words momentarily before she got herself together.

"Your school principal asked me to come and see him in school tomorrow; what have you done this time around?"

CHAPTER 3

Even though Fabian had feigned insensitive the previous day, the chat Mama had with him really touched him, coupled with the fact that the principal summoned her to school. *"How can I make Mama happy with my academics? What did I do that made the school principal summon Mama?"* These questions stole the sleep off his eyes throughout the night; he just couldn't get his head to yield answers. He had hoped that getting Ifiok as his friend will put an end to his academic worries, but Mama just opened a new chapter for him; he must improve his grades. Since he had a sleepless night, he decided to get prepared for school very early, darkness was still lurking around in some hidden places when he was ready for school and left the house, the morning dew was still visible on the leaves and the crickets seemed to be gossiping him, but they became quiet when he passed by. His first knock at the school gate got the security man scrambling to locate the keys.

"Who is there?" He voiced.

"It's Fabian." He unlocked the gate and flung it opened.

"Good morning Mr. Shehu." He could read his facial expression to be *"why is this perpetual late comer here this early*?" Since he didn't answer his greetings and didn't voiced his concern, Fabian immediately walked into the school compound, straight to his class room and on his seat, probably to recover the sleep he couldn't get throughout the night, but the unanswered questions still kept his brain active and drained him till he finally fell asleep. He was only woken by the noise of his classmate returning from the morning devotion.

Immediately Ifiok, Stanley and Musa spotted him inside the class; they ran to him with praises.

"Baddoooo!" They hailed.

"So you were hiding in the class?" Ifiok said while Musa continued the hailing.

"No, I didn't hide."

"Principal was looking for you at the assembly ground and from the look of things, it doesn't seem like he wants to give you a handshake for a job well done." Ifiok said.

This worsened his nervousness, even though he had made up his mind for whatever.

"I think principal has something against us." Fabian said.

"But he saw I, Ifiok and Musa some few minutes ago and didn't say anything." Said a curious Stanley.

"I feel he wants to punish you; but why just you? We have committed all our crimes together. Or did you do anything we don't know about?"

"No. He even summoned my mother to school."

"Why didn't he summon our parents too?" Ifiok asked.

"But what did we do wrong?" Stanley wondered.

"The question should be, were we caught because we broke almost all the rules?" Ifiok corrected.

"No, we were not caught." Musa answered.

"We are always careful when doing our things." Fabian added.

"What if we are just worried over nothing? It might not be punishment." Stanley suggested.

"Yes, you are right. If it was something serious, he would have summoned all of us, because all the rules we broke, we broke them together."

In the midst of their deliberation, a fearful junior student walked into the rowdy class and went straight to where the class captain was seated and whispered something into his ears. Then the class captain stood up, looked around and then spotted Fabian.

"Senior Fabian! Senior Fabian!" The class captain called, mimicking the timid junior student. "Senior Fabian, the principal is calling you."

"Is it just Fabian he's calling?" Musa asked.

"Yes." The junior student timidly answered.

"You see? Go man, it's nothing serious. If it was, all of us would have been summoned." Fabian simply walked out of the class with his heart beating twice faster than normal; his friends tagged along to dampen his fear.

Approaching the principal's office, his friends stayed back while Fabian climbed the pavement to the office block. He heard laughter and people discussing cheerfully in the Principal's office; he ignored it and knocked at the door, since his knock could not stop the discussion, his appearance did. Their eyes observed him from head to toe, then back to head. The two seats opposite the principal were occupied by Mama and his class teacher, Mr. Okafor. Beside the principal's seat was a shelf decorated with trophies. The window was too narrow to allow sufficient sunlight into the office, but one could still see that the office was decorated to fit his position.

"Good morning Mama. Good morning Sir." He took a bow as instructed by their tradition.

"Morning Fabian." The principal replied.

"Fabian, let's start like this; you weren't at the assembly ground this morning?" The principal asked, and Fabian nodded in agreement, and they turned to look at each other.

"I'm sorry. It wasn't intentional. I could not sleep throughout the night, so this morning I was exhausted and I slept off in the class immediately I came." As if that particular crime was forgiven, the principal jumped to the next one.

"What do you go to do outside the school premises during school hours?" He asked.

"I do go to School 2 to play video games and watch movies."

Once again, they looked at each other and Mama covered her face with her hands.

"Is that where I registered you to learn?" Mama asked with low tone.

"No Mama."

"How often do you go there?" The principal asked.

"I go there every day; sometimes after school hours, some other times during school hours."

"And yesterday you went during school hours, right?"

"Yes sir."

"When you go during school hours, how do you leave the school compound since the school gate is always locked?"

"I jumped the school fence."

"I can see how you have been wasting your time. I can see why your academics is suffering and why you've become aggressive. Will it put food on your table? Even if it will, which one should come first, your academics or video game?" The tempo of her voice started rising.

By now, Fabian's eyes were brimming with tears, the deep sense of regret he had been feeling got worse; he was more convinced that he needed a change of attitude towards his academics.

"I'm so sorry Mama; it will never happen again." He promised. He couldn't really tell where that came from, but he knew he has made a promise that he was willing to keep.

"Fabian, if not for the fact that you have shown remorse and sincerity, I would have flogged the heck out of you. You would have been suspended indefinitely and wouldn't have taken part in the forth-coming promotional exams, and that automatically means you would have repeated your present class, and you know what that means - ridicule, mockery and shame. I saw you with my two eyes jumping the school fence yesterday." (The principal opened his eyes to a doom he couldn't bear).

"No sir. No Mama. I don't want to repeat a class. I promise it won't happen again. I promise. Just forgive me this one time; I won't jump any fence again". He broke into tears, rushed to his knees and pleaded. They ignored him as silence filled the atmosphere.

"No offence goes unpunished; so I won't let this slid just like that." The principal broke the silence.

"Sir please, I won't do it again. Mama beg him for me."

"I will flog you 6 strokes." He picked the cane that was close to him, Fabian felt relieved when he heard 6 strokes because he certainly knew that his offence was worth expulsion, and the hope of Mama coming to his rescue was dashed when she said;

"Make it 24 strokes sir.24 strokes!"

"Please madam! He has turned a new live, if not, he knows what we are capable of doing."Mr. Okafor said smiling.

"Ok, I will make it 12 strokes." The principal shifted ground. "Stretch your hand!" He ordered. After the 10th stroke, Fabian caved in as the boy in him conquered and he wailed out begging.

"Mama please don't just sit there, please do something." He completely lost hope when she looked elsewhere. He managed to see his palms, it had blisters all over and the excruciating pain was overwhelming.

"Don't waste my time; two more strokes left."

"This is a slap on the wrist, if you ever repeat such; you will not escape expulsion from this school! Now run to your class." The principal commanded.

Fabian wiped his eyes dry with his uniform, arranged it well and walked into the cheers of Stanley, Ifiok and Musa outside.

"What happened in there? What happened?" They all inquired at the same time.

"Nothing serious, just that the principal saw me when I jumped the fence out of school yesterday, so he gave me 50 strokes of cane and I took it like a man to the amazement of everyone in there." He deceived.

"Wait, how come he saw only you? Ifiok asked.

"You remember I jumped last. Coincidentally, he came out of his office and spotted me when I was about to jump."

"And you covered up for us? Wow!"

"Thanks." They all appreciated him.

"You dusted 50 strokes of cane?" Ifiok asked as if suspecting a lie.

"Then who was wailing in there?" Musa asked.

"Wailing? Did anybody wail?" Fabian asked.

"Yea bro, something like aaaaah, aaaaaah, please sir, Mama please." Stanley demonstrated.

"Well, I don't know. It was definitely not me and definitely didn't come from the principal's office while I was there because we had a matured discussion in there, even as he flogged me 50 strokes." They suspected his lies, but they just let it slid when Mama came out of the principal's office calling Fabian.

"Did your mother come too?" Ifiok asked.

"Yea, she came."

They all walked back to greet her.

"Good morning ma." Ifiok greeted first.

"Morning my sons! How are you all doing?"

"We are all good ma."

"I hope you are prepared for your forth-coming exams?"

"Yes, we are." Ifiok saved the moment.

"I trust you Ifiok."

"Fabian, take this. I made you breakfast since you didn't wait to eat this morning, and also, have this one for lunch." She brought out money from her purse. For whatever reason, Fabian found himself much interested in the money than the food, as he immediately collected the money from her and pocketed it.

"Then, share this with your friends." She gave another sum, but as he was about pocketing it too, Ifiok and Musa held his hand.

"Fabian, oya, share! Share! Share! Don't waste time."

Mama laughed at them.

"Ok. I have to go. You boys should go have fun." Mama said as she departed and they all thanked her for the gift.

"Thank God I have money for my first outing with her."Ifiok stunned them.

"Outing with who?" A curious Musa asked.

"Yes, outing with who?" Stanley added.

Instead of answering them, he kept a mischievous smile, and then, Fabian knew he was serious about Ima Benson.

CHAPTER 4

When they returned to the class, Fabian knew he had to do something very fast about Ima Benson before Ifiok boycotts their agreement. As the rest of the guys started their usual soccer game in class, he disappeared unannounced. After some minutes of play, Ifiok was juggling the soccer paper ball, waiting for Stanley and Musa to restore the post that was scattered by a long shot. A soft hand patted him from behind, not stopping his juggle; he turned and caught a glimpse of Ima Benson. The ball fell on the ground as his legs froze and mouth opened. He was surprised to see her there, not to talk of patting him. He stood there without a word till Ima broke the silence.

"I found this in my bag and it has your name on it." She stretched a Mathematics text book to him, which was truly his."

"Tha...tha...thank...thank you very much." He stammered.

"You are welcome." She answered and walked away.

Few seconds after she left, Ifiok came to his senses and it dawned on him that that was the moment he has been waiting for. "*I must act now.*" He buttoned up his shirt, cleaned the sweat off his face and sanitized himself a little before rushing out of the class with the textbook in his hand to catch up with Ima Benson.

"Excuse me please." He said when he caught up with her. "I am...I am... no sorry, I am Ifiok, and I want to be yo...ur...yo...ur...your friend." He stammered.

"You see, I do not usually stammer, but your presence made me so."

"I understand."

"Please can we study together?" He asked, but she laughed.

"I guess you're just looking for what to say."

"Maybe! Maybe I am star struck."

"Ok. I will think about it and if my thought goes in your favour, I will let you know when I want to study." She said and walked away.

That was the most thrilling event to Ifiok lately, even when she left, he still couldn't move a muscle; he stood there and watched her. When she was finally out of sight, then Stanley and Musa came to him from behind.

"Oh! Someone is in love!" They made jest of him.

"You guys will not understand." He tried to shoo them away, but they wouldn't just leave; as he was about walking back to the class, he spotted Fabian coming from the school cafeteria. He was filled with excitement and was eager to tell him everything that transpired within the last few minutes. He rushed to him with excitement.

"Fabian, you are a genius! You did it!" He jumped on him and hugged him with a crushing force.

"Ifiok, I can't breathe." Fabian managed to say.

"You are a genius!" He finally released him.

"Ok! Calm down and tell me what happened." Fabian played ignorant.

"Ok! Ok! Ok!" Trying to arrange his chain of thoughts.

"We were just in the class playing soccer, then, she came and patted me on the back. Fabian, we talked and I made her laugh. I said I made her laugh, and I even walked her back to her class." He rushed through his sentences.

"Hold your breath man. Who are you talking about?"

"Ima Benson of course. She said she found my text book in her bag, so she came to return it."

"How did your text book get into her bag?" He pretended as if he's not responsible for putting it there.

"I thought you did."

"You must be very smart to think so; now call me a genius again." They all laughed.

"You are a genius!" He hugged him again.

"Yes I know." He said with a smile as they walked back to their class.

Fabian felt impressed with himself and how Ima responded immediately to his plot. Minutes ago, he had disappeared to Ima's classroom with Ifiok's Mathematics textbook and sat close to Ima without saying a word to her. When he noticed Ima was not watching, he carefully placed the textbook in her bag.

So that's how Ifiok and Ima became friends, and since then, Ifiok barely spent time with Fabian; he was always with Ima. Every gist was about Ima. *"Ima this; Ima that."* They were always seen together during and after school hours. Rumors had it that they were dating, but as for Fabian, he just didn't care. Since he couldn't persuade Ifiok to give up his lust for her, he had to find a way to meet his demands; after all, they had an agreement. When Musa and Stanley noticed how much of help Fabian has offered Ifiok to boost his social life, they intensified their query about his interest.

"Fabian, why are you doing all these for this guy?" Musa asked.

"Yes why? First, you made him become our friend and then you *pimped* him up socially, and now, you woo a high class girl for him." Stanley added.

"I'm really under pressure to level up with him academically, and from the look of things, I can't reach him, so it is better I bring him down to my level, and the only way I can do that is to get him distracted. So, if you guys are envious of him, don't be! Nothing I have done is in his own interest; I made him our friend so that we will stop paying him the daily stipend, and that has worked; and now, so that he would be distracted and no longer have time for his studies which would in turn make his academic performance drop. So far, that is working out just well. Haven't you guys noticed he is failing his class works?"

"Wow! That's true. His academics is suffering these days." Musa reasoned.

"Exactly!"

"...And having a girl friend at this point will make his academics suffer more." Stanley added.

"Fabian, you are indeed a genius." Musa concluded.

"Since we cannot reach his level academically, let's bring him down to our academic level; SIMPLE!" Stanley reaffirmed.

"And we must keep this secret away from him." Fabian instructed.

"I think now that he is poor in his academics, let's come up with ways we can top the class this term." Musa suggested.

"That's the spirit. Examination is coming up in two weeks; we just need to prove a point to our parents. Let's top the class this term." Fabian said.

"After all, Ifiok is no more a threat." Musa continued.

"What if we just pretend to be sick and avoid the exam entirely?" Stanley suggested.

"What if we study hard this time?" Musa countered.

"Do you think studying is easy? It's not at all." Stanley
corrected.

"Let's intensify our quest for the magic pen."

"Well, from the look of things, we really need a miracle right
now. Let's go home and think about our chances before we make a
move." Fabian said as they got to a separating point, shook hands
and went in different directions.

These thoughts kept ricocheting in Fabian's mind as he walked
slowly back home. Other students, mostly juniors, scurried passed
him in pairs and groups. Fabian only took just a few steps when a
voice bellowed somewhere behind him, picking up speed to catch up
with him.

"Hey Fabian, where have you been?" Fabian turned.

"Hi Gabriel!" Gabriel was some random guy he met at the game
center.

"Is it because you guys are about to start exams, that's why you
don't come to the game center anymore?"

"Not really, my mother told me to stop coming there."

"Oh! I see."

They walked a bit without saying a word to each other.

"I can help you make distinctions in your exams." Gabriel said.

"How is that possible?"

"There is a man who specializes in helping students succeed in
examinations. He has magic pens he sells, and of course, you know a
magic pen has a life of its own that answers questions the student
cannot answer. With it, you don't need to stay awake all night
studying, you don't need any favour from any teacher to excel. All
you have to do is to buy the pen from the man and all your academic
worries are settled."

"Wow! For real?"

"Yea bro! That's what some of your brilliant students and
teachers use."

"Are you kidding me?"

"Look at you. You better be smart and open your eyes to short
cut."

"Wooow! Gabriel, I have been praying for a miracle to happen
and you brought this good news; Gabriel, you are indeed an angel."

After such revelation by Gabriel, Fabian could not digest the information alone, he went to Musa's and Stanley's houses to intimate them of the development; they assured him of their involvement and mapped out where and when to meet for onward movement to procure the much-needed magic pen. Fabian's desperation to lay his hands on the magic pen made him the first person to arrive at their meeting point. Not long after, Musa and Stanley showed up before Gabriel. They didn't speak much while Gabriel kept embellishing the 'magic pen'.

He told them how the city doctors, professors, teachers, etc., come to the village to buy the pen. Just after some minutes' walk to procure the pen, they got to a mud house with thatched roof; typical of the houses in the village, but the difference was that this particular one looked unkempt. One end of the house had collapsed, and weeds had almost taken over the entire compound. It looked like a place no one had habited for years, but Fabian was surprised when Gabriel said;

"This is where the man lives." Pointing to the house.

"How can a man with the smartest pen on Earth live in this kind of house?" Stanley queried.

"Sssshhhh! He doesn't like noise." Gabriel silenced him.

"Maybe he doesn't like fancy lifestyle." Musa whispered.

"That's not why we are here guys." Fabian whispered back.

Gabriel went to the front door to knock, but when he realized the door could fall off, he clapped instead. An old-stern-looking man came out with white stubble beards; like someone who has known poverty all his life.

"That's the man." Gabriel whispered to them.

They all greeted him in unison, but instead of answering them, the old man observed them from head to toe, one after the other.

"Are these the students you told me about?" He asked Gabriel with a baritone voice.

"Yes Baba." Gabriel answered as Fabian and his gang nodded aimlessly like a lizard that fell from a height.

"I won't do it." His response was harsh and shocked them to their bones and marrows.

"But Baba why?"

"I won't do it for them, he turned to leave, but Gabriel doubled crossed him immediately to beg as others joined.

"Please Baba, consider these ones for my sake; they don't have anywhere else to go for help." Gabriel begged.

"Please sir, if you don't do it for us, we will all fail the exam." After seconds of consideration, Baba agreed to sell the pen to them.

"Ok. I will, but you must promise not to tell anyone about it."

"We promise. We won't." They chorused.

"If you do, you would be paralyzed." Gabriel demonstrated the paralyzed movement.

"We won't Baba."

"And you have to pay twice the price."

Doubling the price did not matter to them; they paid and got the magic pen. It was an exciting thing to them as they were fully ready for the coming examinations, and kept it as a secret from Ifiok.

<hr>

The atmosphere had being tensed since the commencement of the examination, as some students lost a few kg due to rigorous studying. After every paper, they assembled in groups or pairs to discuss the questions they answered or didn't answer, before they dispersed to prepare for the next paper. Gabriel, had told Fabian and his friends not to worry, but scribble anything on their answer booklet to avoid suspicion. He said the miracle of the magic pen will not be seen by its user in the examination hall, but the examiner will see the right answers when marking the script and give them high scores. That was exactly what they did, in some examinations they copied the questions to the answer booklet and submitted.

Some examiners thought Fabian and his gang were getting answers from Ifiok, so in an attempt to burst them, they relocated Ifiok from the back seat to the front of the class where no one could interact with him. None of them really bothered about it; after all, Ifiok had nothing better to offer as he was also struggling with simple class works.

"How was it?" Ifiok would always ask after each exam.

Their answers were always a positive monosyllabic word, without letting him know about their little magic pen.

"You guys seem to be doing very well; I mean, you finished and submitted before anyone else." Ifiok said.

"Yes, we discovered a secret, one we don't want to share with you." Musa answered.

"If he is really interested in knowing, you can tell him, after all, we have just 2 exams left." Fabian said.

"Well, there is this pen we bought, it has been helping us answer questions; it answers all our questions."

"Is it magic pen?"

"Yes."

"Wow! Why didn't you guys tell me about this pen?" They looked at each other without knowing what to say.

"To be honest and blunt with you, we didn't tell you because we want you to fail this time around."

"But why? I thought we were friends." Even though Ifiok had seen this possibility, the revelation still made him feel sad.

"We are not friends; we don't like you and will probably never like you."

"So you guys have been pretending to be my friend all along?"

"Yes."

Somehow, Ifiok got emotional, but tried to put it under control and act tough.

"Well, I also got my magic pen and didn't want to tell you guys about it too." They looked shocked.

"Your magic pen is not as good as ours because you are still reading for each exam." Stanley said.

"Ok then, let's see whose magic pen works better." Ifiok said.

CHAPTER 5

The judgment day finally came, as every student in SS1 gathered at the front of the staff room, waiting for Mr. Okafor to show up with their results. When he finally came, he gave an address that gladdened Fabian's hearts.

"As you all know, after the examination comes the results; I have your results right here in my hands. I am very proud of you all. Give yourselves a round of applause." The students gave a resounding applause.

"Most of you have done extremely well; you have taken the bull by the horn and improved in your academics. I am very proud of you all." He ended his pep talk with his gaze rested on Fabian who stood alone at the back of the crowd.

"Mr. Okafor must have noticed my improvement academically. I know I must have fallen in the category of students that he was talking about." Fabian thought to himself

Fabian patiently waited as Mr. Okafor started calling out the names on the result for collection. He didn't wait for long as Mr. Okafor called out four names at a stretch, and Fabian's name was amongst, but before he could get to the front and get it, the class captain had collected the result and indiscriminately say;

"This is yours; this is yours."

Without checking the names, the class captain mixed up the results while handing it to them. Fabian collected his supposed result and walked away from the crowd; his face lightened up and his eyes glowed when he unfolded the result. Just as he expected; English A1, Biology A1, Mathematics A1, Physics B2, etc.

"Yes! Yes! Yes!" He punched the air in excitement. "At last, I have made it. The magic pen is indeed a miracle." While concentrating on his eight distinctions, he started walking slowly to the class to get his bag and go home, so as to show Mama at once.

"Fabian! That is my result you are holding, and this is yours." A familiar voice said.

Fabian looked up and it was Ifiok; he tried to shield the result from Ifiok.

"Yes, it's my result. Look at my name on it." Ifiok insisted, and for the first time since Fabian was given the result, he looked at the name written on it; it wasn't his name. He cleared his eyes, hoping it will change to his name, but *Ifiok Cyril Akpan* refused to go away.

"This is yours." Ifiok stretched another to him; it was a replica of his former result, the only thing written with blue ink was just his name, *Fabian Okon*; the grades where F9 all through.

For a moment, his life came to a standstill; with his mouth glued, all he could do was to stare at both result sheets in comparison; the difference was too great.

Ifiok gently collected his own result from him and walked away.

Fabian was shattered; his feet couldn't carry his weight anymore as he dropped on his knees.

Stanley and Musa showed up from the crowd; their faces said it all. They peeped at Fabians result; it was a replica of theirs, as they sat on the ground.

"Gabriel has some explanations to do." Stanley said.

"Yes! Let's go see him at once." Musa concurred.

They immediately went to School 2 where he was always seen, but on that day, he was nowhere to be found, not even a trace of him. So, they extended their search to Baba's house in the next village. No one was there. They asked the people living in the neighbourhood who revealed to them no one lived in the compound, and that it has been an abandoned building for many years. That alone confirmed their fears. "They were scammed!"

~

Since Fabian and his friends could not reach Gabriel, Fabian quietly left for home to go face whatever ordeal awaited him. He knew there would be a lot of backlashes and tension from Mama throughout the holiday. The thought of dousing the tension his result will cause struck him, but he was not sure if it would change Mama's position when she sees his result; he had to try, so he increased his pace. Upon getting home, he noticed Mama was not back from the farm yet; he immediately opened Mama's room, dropped his bag on the bed with his result popping out and started cleaning and tidying up the room, just so Mama will appreciate and give him a soft landing.

When he was done sweeping the entire compound and trimming the flowers outside, he returned to Mama's room to fetch his school bag only to discover Mama had returned, sitting on the bed, focusing on his result. His greetings were of no value to her, and the much anticipated appreciation for the chores he had done was not forthcoming, so he decided to sing his praises.

"Mama the plates I washed are still dripping water, should I dry them under the sun?" He waited for her response, but no word came from her and he continued;

"Mama while sweeping the floor, I noticed some tiny ants were coming out of the ground, but I ignored them and swept everywhere including your room." Still, no word from her.

"Mama, I fetched water and firewood; now I want to wash your clothes, please if you have more clothes bring them for me to wash." She finally gave him the snub of his life and walked out of the room. Mama had seen his result and his trick failed him. He started plotting his next line of action when he noticed someone walked into the compound. He became furious when he noticed it was Ifiok, he immediately stormed outside and pushed him.

"You again? So you have come to ridicule me like you did in school, huh?" He pushed him again.

"Fabian, what are you doing?" Mama's voice from behind froze him before he could cause more damage.

"Oh Ifiok my son, don't mind him. Come inside! Come in, come in." Ifiok made gesture for Fabian to make way for him; Fabian obstructed him and folded his fist.

"Fabian!" Mama called out again before Fabian came back to his senses and gave in.

"Oh my son, you are welcome. She embraced Ifiok and ushered him into her room.

"Fabian, come and get Ifiok something to drink."

"There is nothing for him to drink." he thundered but Mama ignored it

"I made orange juice, get it from the kitchen." Fabian grumbled and grudgingly did what he was told.

"How are your parents, Ifiok?" Mama asked.

"They are fine."

"That's good to know. Do I need to ask about your academic performance this term, I'm sure you surpassed the previous ones?" Ifiok was shy to maintain eye contact with her; Mama gazed at Fabian with a mocking eye as he returned with the cup of homemade juice.

"Well, Mama, as it has always been our tradition, I came to show you my result." Ifiok brought out his result and showed to Mama.

"Oh my son, you have done very well. You have made us proud, especially your parents. May God bless you my son." Fabian lost count of the number of times Mama called Ifiok her son and that worsened his jealousy. He didn't know when he cried out;

"Mama, Ifiok is not your son; I'm the only son you have." Fabian outburst jolted them. He managed to give him the drink and stayed in the room to hear if Ifiok will say something damaging about him.

"I wish some people put in this level of commitment into their school work too." She jabbed at Fabian.

"They will very soon; from next term, things will change for the better."

"I pray o..." Fabian felt really nice to hear Ifiok defend him at least.

"Let me leave you two to catch along, I will be back soon." Mama stood and left. Silence filled the room for a while before Ifiok said something;

"Fabian, I actually came here to see you." Ifiok said.

"For what? To ridicule me in front of Mama?"

"Fabian relax; that's not why I'm here. I noticed how disappointed you were after seeing your result; how you stared at mine, wishing it was yours. Fabian there is no such thing as magic pen, and there is no shortcut to success. Every day, I spend time studying, and I invest in reading materials; what I don't know, I ask people that are ahead of me. I instill in myself this burning desire to stay on top and this yielded the result you saw some moments ago."

"What are you talking about?"

"There is no shortcut to success and there is no substitute to hard work. Fabian, magic pen was clearly a fraud, and I thank God you have learnt your lessons." Ifiok replied.

"Fabian, prioritize your life; doing well in school should be your top priority. Study hard; there is no magic pen that can substitute it. Always attend classes; ignore school 2 in its entirety. Do all your homework and develop self-discipline." Ifiok advised.

"Manage your time; once you do, academic success will not elude you." He added.

"Your result surprised me; for the first time, you had a distinction in Mathematics."

"Yes! You know I was too shy to talk to girls. I accepted your friendship offer so you would help me woo Ima, and she would help me improve in my Mathematics; and you know Ima is the goddess of Mathematics. Another reason I accepted your friendship offer is to influence you positively."

"So, that's it? You used me all along?"

"Yes. But in a different way you were using me." Ifiok replied.

"See, I know about your plot; how you tried to distract me academically. You did this so you can surpass me during exams. I tell you what, you don't need to pull anyone down, because there is room for everyone who is willing to put in extra effort. Success is not for selected people; it's for everyone - you and I. Join me, and we would succeed together."

"You knew all these, why didn't you tell me all along?"

"I was supposed to, but when I remembered how you guys have been mistreating and bullying me, I thought I should allow you guys learn the hard way."

"As a payback huh? You are wicked."

"Hahaha! Look at who is talking about being wicked."

"See, it's glaring you want a better academic performance, am I right?"

"Yes Ifiok. If not for anything, for the sake of Mama; she has not said a word to me since she saw my result."

"Good! Since you already know what you want, connect with like minds; people that want the same thing. See, Ima and I came together to form a study group to prepare ourselves for the forth-coming inter-school competition. I want you to be part of that study group."

"Are you for real?"

"Yea bro!"

Mama came out with a gift for Ifiok to appreciate his academic excellence.

"Mama, I'm off to study with Ifiok." Fabian said. He couldn't dwell in his ignorance for yet another minute, so immediately Ifiok handed him the offer to join his study group, he jumped at it. He didn't move an inch away from him; he followed Ifiok to his house to get his study materials before they proceeded to the study center.

They got there before Ima; Fabian had a feeling she was going to be uncomfortable with his presence because she might have heard a fair sheer of his stubbornness, but the reverse was the case. She was excited and welcoming when she arrived. They usually met and studied at the village's uncompleted town hall which was left unattended, and weeds took over, but when Ifiok made it as their choice place to study, he took time to clear the weeds and made it habitable.

"Hi Fabian! So good to see you; Are you joining us?" Ima asked with all smiles, and Fabian nodded affirmatively. "That's a wise decision then. Let's get started." She went to the writing board Ifiok had constructed.

"For Fabian's sake, I will start this topic from the scratch again." *"She is really the Mathematics goddess; if she isn't, she wouldn't have won all the laurels she won for herself and the school."* Fabian thought to himself. She often stopped from time to time to ask if Fabian understood, and it was a lot easier for him to tell her he didn't understand because they were peers. It was interactive. When Ifiok took over from her, Fabian realized he had a lot of learning to do because they used terms he wasn't familiar with. Sometimes, they spent time to break it down to his understanding. After the class, Ima walked up to Fabian and asked;

"How did you see the lesson?"

"It was insightful. Thank you."

"You are welcome."

"But how do you know so much?" Fabian enquired.

"I know so much because I study so much."

"How long will it take me to know all what you know?"

"Don't sweat it Fabian, just keep learning; bring your friends along. Collaboration helps learning and learning regularly improves our brain capability, which makes one smart, sharp and active."

"I really wish you can follow us to the annual Exxon Mobil Inter-school Competition." Ifiok said.

"Even represent our school." Ima concurred.

"Do you guys think I'm good enough?"

"Yea."

CHAPTER 6

As the holiday came and gone; Fabian came to appreciate the beauty of learning with like minds, the improvement in his school work made him believe he was never a dullard; he was only paying attention to the wrong things. He invited Musa and Stanley to join them, but it seemed they were not ready for the inevitable change, so he had no choice than to plan his new future without them.

His relationship with Mama back home improved significantly; once again, he became her source of hope and happiness, and his meal each time was garnished with all sorts of meats and fish. Her partnership with his school management became even stronger.

~

One day, Fabian was called to come to the principal office, since he knew he had not committed any offence, he went there boldly. He was stunned to see Mama, his teachers and the principal; they were all in a cheerful mood. Definitely, they were not discussing the village politics or the price of palm oil in the local market; they were discussing him.

"Oh here he is." The principal said.

"I know you are surprised to see your mother here."

Fabian nodded with a smile.

"Don't be my son. It's the right thing to do. Parents should collaborate and build synergy with the teachers; join the Parents' Teachers' Association and interact; just as your mother is doing. She is a very nice woman." The principal said.

Fabian understood where the compliment was coming from when he noticed the brown envelopes in their hands.

"See Fabian, I have been receiving good reports about your performance this term and I want to encourage you not to relent."

"Ok sir."

"I must say, since the beginning of this term, he is now a better person, character wise." Mr. Okafor contributed.

"Wow! That's good. If you continue on this path, you will achieve greatness. In fact, you will be recommended for competitions." The principal said.

"Principal, I really want to thank the school management once again for your contribution." Mama said.

"You should also appreciate him, because our people say, you can take a thirsty cow to the stream, but you cannot force it to drink."

"Yes, exactly."

~

The day of the Exxon Mobil Inter-school Competition finally came; Ifiok and Ima had prepared thoroughly, and the school management selected the best students from each class to accompany them; to stay in the audience and cheer them to success. It never bothered Fabian why he wasn't chosen, but he was ready to give Ifiok all the support he could get. So, on that day, he left the sun in bed to have a full dose of its sleep, while he took his bath, wore his uniform and went straight to Ifiok's house. It was never their plan to meet that morning though. Getting there, Ifiok was bent, lacing his shoes, ready to leave, while his parents sat on the bamboo bench holding the kerosene lantern for their 15 year son to see his way. Even in such dark early hours, Fabian could still notice the wrinkles on their skin, no need to say that poverty was a communal phenomenon. When Fabian was spotted, Ifiok took a break from his shoe lacing and stood upright. Ifiok's mother stood up as Fabian went straight to her and gave a hug, then shook his father with two hands, acknowledging how rough and hard his palms were.

"You are welcome my son." Ifiok's mother greeted with a smile.

"Are you also going with them?" Ifiok father asked.

"No. I'm not going. I just came to make sure Ifiok does not bring his big head home without a crown." Ifiok's parents laughed.

With a smile, Fabian and Ifiok's eyes locked for a moment; they had developed a fast growing bond.

"I really wish you can come with us." They broke eye contact. He bent again to finish up his shoe lace.

"Naa man, it's not my thing."

"Ok, let's get going." Ifiok said as they head to the exit of the compound

"Bye bye!" Ifiok's parents greeted; waving at them as they departed.

The fortune of Fabian knowledge had grown in lips and bounds, due to hard work, but not enough to be taken out for such a competition that would be broadcasted live on TV. The school management knew it was an expensive risk they couldn't take.

As they started walking to the meeting point which was apparently their school; they talked and threw jabs at each other as if they've been friends for years. By the time they got to school, the sun was just waking up, and the birds were singing its praises. The driver was seen trying to clean the mini bus the school hired. Fabian and Ifiok stood aside and continued their never ending gist, no one could really say what they were talking about, but they busted into laughter from time to time.

After some minutes, other students arrived. When Ima came, she looked and sounded dull; Fabian and Ifiok could notice all was not right, as she only managed to wave at them before mounting the bus; leaving them to deliberate on her mood.

"What happened to her?" Ifiok asked.

"I should be asking you."

"Ifiok, what are you still doing outside?" Mr. Okafor queried; then it dawned on Fabian they were about leaving. So, they shook hands as Ifiok matched towards the bus. Mr. Okafor looked inside the bus as if to have a head count.

"Two people are not here; who are they?" Mr. Okafor asked.

The students mentioned the names of the *yet-to-come* students and gave reasons they were not available. Without a second thought, Mr. Okafor gestured to Fabian to come to him. Fabian looked behind to see if he was really talking to him.

"Fabian come here!" He finally called out.

"Get inside the bus; let's go."

"Sir, there is a mistake somewhere." Fabian countered.

"No mistake."

"Sir, I'm not among those coming with you. In fact, I'm not even supposed to be here at all." He was about walking away when Mr. Okafor held him.

"You are coming now; so enter the bus."

"But Mama is unaware."

"I will send a message to her right now." Mr. Okafor countered.

"Sir, I have Fever and Diarrhea." Ifiok and the other students in the bus laughed out loud.

"I know you have Fever and Diarrhea, that's why you must follow us to that competition to see a doctor."

The few excuses couldn't let Fabian off the hook, and he knew his mother would definitely consent to his involvement in such a high profile competition, so he reluctantly walked into the bus. For no particular reason, he took the seat beside Ima. Mr. Okafor slid the door to a close, and then went to the front seat of the bus, told the driver to move and they set out for the competition.

Inside the bus, Fabian tried not to look at Ifiok because he noticed he had started making fun of him, but when their eyes coincidentally met, he could not help but smile back; Ifiok's wish for him to be taken along finally came to fulfillment. Ima was still moody; not willing to talk to anyone. She bent forward and rested her head on the back of the seat opposite her. So, Fabian completely ignored her and focused his attention on anything he could see outside the window of the moving bus. The bus was a rare sight in a village like *IkotObong Akan*, so as they journeyed through the village, the kids couldn't hide their excitement that morning. Some ran after the bus, while some waved at them. The elders shouted prayers of blessings and protection. As they progress into the city, the bad sandy road slowly became a tarred one, the road side bushes were replaced by houses and the road side cassava farms were no more, instead flowers were used to beautify the most houses. When they got to the venue of the competition in *Uyo*, the state capital, they alighted from the bus. Fabian took few seconds to comprehend the gigantic three-storied building that would accommodate them for some hours. The first of such a building he has ever seen in his entire life, same with most of the students. It was adorned with beautiful lightings of bright colours and beautiful decorations that almost eclipsed the whole building.

Other schools had arrived before them, and from their appearance, school bus and polished English, Fabian could easily notice the affluence; obviously, they were from one of the expensive private schools for the rich in the city.

Mr. Okafor ceased the opportunity for a pep talk.

"Listen guys, we're not here just to honour the invitation, but to prove to everyone that there are sound students in rural schools! We've done it before, and we can do it again." He said.

"Ima, am I right?" Mr. Okafor asked, and Ima timidly nodded.

"Good. So, keep your eyes on the prize. What did I say?"

"Keep your eyes on the prize." They all chorused.

"Ok! Good. Now, let's go."

They were received into the hall as kings and queens by some beautiful smiling ushers who led them to their seats. The hall was quite beautiful, with cinematic lightings, and the seats introduced them to comfort. Once again, Fabian found himself sitting beside Ima and he was determined to start a conversation with her this time around.

"Hey, I'm beside you again." He smilingly said, but she only looked at him without saying a word. Then, he noticed her trembling hands and sweaty forehead.

"This is stage fright." Fabian whispered to himself.

Ima lost her self-confidence before they got there, but no one noticed. Her nervousness became obvious; few minutes after they got seated, she took permission from Mr. Okafor and went to the rest room.

When every invited school had settled, the Moderator took to the stage with a microphone in his hand. He pressed a button on the microphone, tapped it twice and it amplified the sound before he moved it closed to his mouth.

"Ladies and gentlemen, boys and girls; my name is Steve Melson and I would be your moderator for today With all due respect, I will like to welcome you all to this year's *EXXON MOBIL INTER-SCHOOL QUIZ COMPETITION."* His deep baritone voice resonated in the hall and accentuated his captivating presence.

Steve Melson was a renowned TV presenter; every student in the hall seemed to know him, except Fabian and his colleagues from the village. He looked classy in his well-tailored suit and shiny shoes; his diction was well-polished like that of a movie star. He said a joke; it was either the crowd didn't get it or the joke wasn't funny, but one thing was certain, no one laughed; but when he asked them to clap for themselves, the hall came alive. The applause rescinded before the host started calling out the names of the participating schools, and their representatives moved in pairs to the designated rostrum at the front hall. At this point, Mr. Okafor became restless.

"Where is Ima? Why is she not back yet?" He asked.

"She went to the rest room." Ifiok answered.

"It's taking too long."

"She must have absconded" Fabian thought to himself. *"If my instinct serves me right, Mr. OKAFOR will definitely look for a replacement, and who could that be?"* He wondered.

The fear of him going up there in front of those people made his adrenaline pump faster.

"Sir, let me go and look for her, and bring her here at once." Fabian volunteered to help.

"No! Stay where you are." That was how his escape plan was truncated.

As he was thinking about his next escape plan;

"IkotObong Akan Community High School!" The moderator called out.

"Fabian, you will go with Ifiok to the rostrum." Came Mr. Okafor's voice. Fabian eyes widened; his heart sank and his brain stopped working.

"Sir, remember I said I have Fever and Diarrhea."

"Yes, I remember so well; this is your ticket to seeing a doctor."

Before he could lodge another complain, one of their colleagues pointed to Ima coming from behind. He breathed a sigh of relief and Mr. Okafor rushed her to the stage, without acknowledging the panic attack.

As Ifiok and Ima walked to the rostrum, they looked defeated already, but Mr. Okafor started clapping and everyone joined to cheer them up. The applause only stopped when they were fully positioned in front of the rostrum that had the name of their school.

"Wow! I know the distance you travelled to get here was tiring, but lift up your spirit with that applause." The moderator said before calling out two more schools to the rostrum, then kick-started the competition.

"Once again, I welcome you all to this year's Exxon Mobil Inter-school Quiz Competition. This competition is an annual ritual that seeks to appreciate the hard working schools, and reward the students that mirror such schools." He kept quiet in a way that showed he wanted the audience to clap. Without failing, he got the cue and gave a thunderous round of applause.

"Right here on this podium, we have selected 10 schools represented by two of their students. Every question they answer correctly gives them 2points." He explained, and he went further to read out the rules and regulations of the competition, after which the competition began.

When the competition started, Fabian couldn't believe his eyes as the all-knowing Ifiok and Ima had missed the first 5 questions; his school was really lagging behind while other schools had garnered 10 to 12 points. Ifiok was stammering and unsure of everything coming out of his mouth, and Fabian began to think maybe he had been infected with Ima's stage fright as well.

But somehow, they struggled to get their first 3 points, and then got just enough points to escape the elimination round.

The next round was quite different, Ifiok rose to the occasion and his school started getting the right answers. Ima gained her confidence and rose to the occasion too, but they were still trailing behind other schools. Fabian embraced reality; they were no way getting close to the 1st prize, and he took solace in the fact that even if they didn't win, he had learned something, and the experience would live with him forever.

While he was thinking of how he would brag about his experience to Mama, one of the contesting schools chose a question number they couldn't answer within the allotted time, the moderator awarded the question as a bonus to any school with the right answer, yet, none of them could offer the right answer. He then threw the question open to the audience, but no one seems to know the answer.

"What is a disease-causing organism called?"

"Pathogen!" Unconsciously, the word came out of Fabian's mouth. It was never his intention to be heard.

"Who said Pathogen?" Asked the moderator, fear gripped Fabian, and he tried to hide his face, but those that heard him turned and looked his direction. He felt himself sinking lower and lower in his chair. If the ground had opened at that time, he would have gladly jumped in and disappeared.

"Stand up my friend." The moderator said, and the whole hall went silent. Fabian could hear his heart running out of its chambers;

it was too late, the moderator had identified him; he timidly stood up.

"What did you say the answer is?" He queried again.

"Pa, pa pathogen!" He stammered.

"Yes! You are correct. A round of applause for him!"

For the first time in his life, he stood up to give a correct answer to a question and received applause. The feeling was awesome and the applause was deafening. His timid face changed into a smile. Then, he remembered the saying that one should always celebrate his achievements, no matter how small. This became his proudest moment as a student and he got lost in it; he stood there enjoying the euphoria of the moment with a smile on, unconsciously, he started waving at the applauding students, thanking them.

"Thank you! Thank you! Thank you!" Blowing kisses to them. The crowd busted into laughter and the applause became louder; his eyes rested on Ifiok and they wink at each other.

"I can imagine how you are feeling right now, like some top politician or a super star waving at his fans." The moderator said smilingly when the applause rescinded.

"Of course yes, like the president of this country." Fabian replied.

"But you sounded like you were not sure initially."

"Well, I was about asking you if that's all you got sir."

"Now, see who is bragging."

"I mean it sir."

"That sounds like a challenge and I will be glad to burst your bubbles." The moderator smilingly said.

The moderator looked to his left and right then said;

"Ladies and gentlemen, boys and girls and everyone watching us at home, please permit me to break our usual protocol and do what has never been done on this show. What's your name?"

"Fabian Okon."

"Ok. Fabian Okon, I will ask you 5 questions and if you are able to answer them correctly without missing anyone. I will host you in my TV show *EDUCATION LIVE*; how about that?"

"Sounds cool to me."

"No live lines whatsoever, no options given, no call a friend, no whispering and no side talk. In fact come out to the front and stand.

This will not go in favour or against any of the competing schools. It's just between you and I...Ok?"

"Bring it on sir!"

"I like your spirit young man; that applause just took your confidence to a whole new level."

"Thank you sir." He walked to the front of the audience as said by the moderator.

"My first question to you is; mention 5 Noble Peace Prize Laureate from Africa?"

"Abiy Ahmed of Ethiopia, Albert Lithuli of South Africa, Anwar Al-sadat of Egypt, Nelson Mandela of South Africa and Kofi Anan of Ghana."

"Brilliant! A round of applause for Fabian."

"I was hoping you will ask me what a Nobel Peace Prize is." He said when the applause rescinded.

"No, I read widely."

"That's good."

The moderator went on to ask the 2nd, 3rd and 4th questions, which they all happen to be things Fabian knew and he gladly provided the right answers. The 5th question came to him as a surprise;

"Who can we attribute this quote to *'Education is the passport to the future, for tomorrow belongs to those who prepare for it today'*?" Fabian smiled for a moment; *"That's the same quote that serves as my mother's anthem whenever she is advising me."* He thought to himself as the moderator repeated the question.

"Who can we attribute this quote to *'Education is the passport to the future, for tomorrow belongs to those who prepare for it today'*?"

"My mother." Fabian finally said.

"Your Mother? For real? Try again son."

"That's my mother's favourite quote."

"Ok."

"The answer to your question is Malcolm X; he was an African-American human rights activist born in May 19, 1925 in Omaha, Nebraska, USA to a woman named Louise Norton Little and died on February 21, 1965."

"Well, I don't know what else to say, YOU ARE 100% RIGHT." The moderator yelled.

As if they have won the competition itself, Mr. Okafor and all *IkotObong Akan Community School* students went into wild celebration and everyone in the audience followed suit.

"Fabian Okon, you would be my guest on 'EDUCATION LIVE', a 30-minute show on TV to help sanitize the education sector." One of the ushers walked to the stage and handed a note to the moderator.

"...and information reaching me right now says a good samaritan has made a generous donation of 1million Naira for your educational advancement."

Again, Mr. Okafor led the audience into a wild celebration.

"Whew! Fabian what a show you have turned this into. What a day for you my friend. I have moderated this competition for 10 consecutive years; I must confess, this is the best ever. The same usher brought another piece of paper to the moderator.

"FABIAN OKON, another viewer at home has pledged the sum of 1million Naira to your academic pursuit." The moderator rushed to hug and carry him; the staff and students rushed at him, as Ifiok and Mr.Okafor joined, carrying and tossing him up.

"Ok! Ok! Please, we must continue our regular quiz. Please settle down." The moderator shouted into the microphone after minutes of celebration, bringing the celebration to a halt.

"IkotObong Akan Community High School, I don't know where you got this genius from; Fabian, thank you for inspiring us all. You can   go   back   to   your   seat."

CHAPTER 7

It was evening before the 2 buses got to *IkotObong Akan;* the villagers had returned from their farms and preparing for dinner when the buses drove in, blaring horn as siren, as the students in it sang, clapped and chanted; *"We have won!"* The villagers who didn't get the message were alarmed, wondering what was happening, until the good news got to the four corners of the village. *"They went in one bus and came back in two buses."* Most of them thought. The gateman who heard them coming from a distance flung the school gate open as the busses cornered into the deserted school compound. The school had closed and all students had gone home, but they all resurfaced in their mufti when they heard the triumphant entry of their representatives. Mr. Okafor and his team alighted from the buses when they were brought to a halt by the drivers; into the warmed embrace of the school principal who waited for their arrival.

The school drummers rushed into the principal's office and brought out drums, and in no time, an assembly was conducted. The school assembly was turned into a festival of some sort, welcoming parents and well-wishers from all the corners of the village who trooped into the school en-mass to see for themselves the brand new 18-seater bus won for the school, and how Ifiok and Ima would be offered scholarship certificate to study in any higher institution of their choice.

"Yes, we won! Yes, we won!" Was the chant everywhere.

~

Indeed, they won the competition, but not without a tide with Gloryland Academy who prolonged the competition to a knockout stage that meant all questions must be answered correctly. Ifiok and Ima put up a scintillating performance which gave them a narrow win, after Gloryland Academy failed to answer one of the questions.

Almost all the villagers were present at the assembly ground; singing, dancing and clapping, where necessary. For no known reason, Ifiok was not in their midst. He sat in an adjacent empty classroom and watched the on-going celebration. Fabian was the life of the party; everyone had a congratulatory message to offer him. As if that was not enough, they carried him and tossed him into the air, chanting; *"We have won! We have won! We have won!"* and he seemed to be enjoying it all. Ifiok only smiled at him, he was filled with satisfaction, knowing he had made monumental strides in Fabian's life. He picked up his bag and set to go home before Fabian reached for him unexpectedly.

"Hey! What are you doing here all alone?"

"Hey! Nothing actually... Maybe I want a better view of this moment."

"Thank you." Fabian said.

"For what?"

"Don't act like you don't know you really influenced me positively. You know if the events of these few weeks had happened in a movie, you would have been the hero of such movie."

"I wonder who the villain would have been." Ifiok said, and Fabian looked at him suspiciously before they started laughing.

"Relax my friend; we will share the heroic role." They got quiet momentarily.

"Fabian, I know a lot of people have told you how proud you have made them, let me join the list. I AM VERY PROUD OF YOU."

"No, You are actually the star of the moment; I'm just helping you live it since you're too modest." They maintained a lull.

"I'm really sorry for all the troubles I caused you before."

"Never mind." They shook hands and locked eyes.

"Boys! Pardon me; I will have to interrupt this moment." The principal said as he approached them and they stood properly.

"Mr. Okafor has briefed me on how you Ifiok put up a scintillating performance, how you Fabian made new rich friends and Ima was outstanding as usual; you guys have made this school very popular and I want you to know that the school management appreciates you and will urge you to continue on that path; I can tell there is greatness for each of you."

"Ok sir." They both said.

"Follow me boys, let's go to the assembly ground."

The principal led them out of the class, into the field. The two boys got excited when they saw their parent walking toward them

"Have we missed anything yet?" Their parents covered Fabian and Ifiok in a hug.

"We have heard the story and we are proud of you boys." Ifiok's father spoke as loud as possible.

"These boys are incredible, look at the brand new bus they won for the school." The principal said, pointing to the bus, before he spotted Ima and immediately called her to come over.

"These are the 3 geniuses that made it happen." The principal introduced Ima to them when she got to them. After, they showered them with praises.

"Please come along; I need to address my student and everyone." The principal led them to the crowd, and then pushed his way through it. He mounted the pavement that served as a stage while Fabian, Ifiok and Ima are left in the crowd. He signaled to the drummers to stop and a relative decorum was maintained.

"My dear people of *IkotObong Akan,* I want to thank you all for abandoning your evening activities and coming out to celebrate this day with us, and also, I want to thank my students that had gone home before for coming out too. Permit me to officially declare to you; YES! *IkotObong Akan High School* came first in this year's Exxon Mobil competition." The crowd was about going into a jubilation, but he signaled them to remain calm as he continued."...and that brand new 18-seater bus you see right there" He pointed at the bus, "would not have been ours without these geniuses, Ifiok and Ima please join me here." He beckoned to them.

"Look at these two great students; they are the symbols of greatness of this citadel of learning. Year after year, they have won laurels for this school, and this year is not an exception. They have never allowed their achievements to get into their heads, instead, they get better with each passing year. My students, there are many of you still lagging behind academically, I want you all to emulate their good virtues. Make friends with them; make friends with people that are ahead of you, they will help you grow. Approach us your teachers and ask questions; that is one key ingredient Fabian came to understand. Fabian, come up here." Fabian, smiling, climbed up the pavement. "You all know Fabian; he was a lazy student. He never liked school; just like many of you here, he never liked studying, but here he is today, we are celebrating him. How did he get it right, you might ask me; first he was determined to improve his academics, second, he made friends with people that are ahead of him academically, and lastly, he sowed the seed of hard work; that is why we have come here to celebrate him."

"From Fabian's story, you can see that you might have started on the wrong footing, but you can still find your way academically, just like Fabian."

"And to you parents here, I know how Fabian's mother was genuinely pushing for his success; don't just leave your wards for the teachers alone. We are all partners in building these children. Come to school from time to time to know how your children are doing, having your children in school goes beyond payment of fees. Build a relationship with the school management."

Lastly, my students, I know school is not everything, but school is something; a citadel of learning, where you are molded with abilities to face future challenges. So, since you have the opportunity to be in school, take it seriously; not just for the good grades, but for the knowledge and skills... I'm expecting big things from you all; don't fail me. I really don't have much to say, CONGRATULATIONS." He turned and shook Fabian firmly; "Remember me when you go to cash out." He jokingly said, then Mr. Okafor who was standing close by, presented the new bus key and scholarship certificates to the Principal and he handed the certificate to Ifiok and Ima with a handshake before showing them the way down the pavement.

He then cleared his throat before waving the Bus key to the crowd and the drummers started playing. The crowd that was initially calm went wild in celebration again as they dispersed. Some went to catch a glimpse of the new bus.

Fabian found his way through the crowd to his joyous mother.

"Mama, why is it that after talking for so long, you guys still end up saying 'I really don't have much to say'?" Referring to the principal.

"We guys?"

"Yes. You old people." She jokingly moved closer to him with a spank and he drifted away from her till she started chasing him on the school field laughing.

———

So, the once lazy and unserious Fabian found his bearing academically, and moved from the back to the front. That moment became a new beginning for him; a new dawn to turn things around for the woman who sacrificed all for him and his future; a time to set himself up for greater things ahead. The future was bright and shiny for him and he was ready to go for it.

After winning the competition, the trio stuck together and continued their study group till Ifiok and Ima finished as the best graduating students in their respective years, and went ahead to secure a scholarship to study in any university of their choice, while Fabian graduated with all round distinctions and came to agree with Mama that *"Education is the passport to the future, and tomorrow belongs to those who prepare for it today."*

ABOUT THE AUTHOR

Emmanuel J. Nkanang is a freelance writer from Nigeria, but resides in United Arab Emirate. When he is not writing short stories for teenagers, he writes plays. His plays have been performed in schools and churches, and his articles have also appeared on magazines. Emmanuel is a former facilitator of AEI Book Club and he is a staunch believer that good books can be used to plant good seeds in the minds of the little ones.